This book belongs to
_____

This book is dedicated to my children - Mikey, Kobe, and Jojo.

Copyright © 2023 Grow Grit Press LLC. All rights reserved. No part of this book may be reproduced in any form without permission in writing from the publisher. Please send bulk order requests to info@ninjalifehacks.tv

Paperback ISBN: 978-1-63731-635-1
Hardcover ISBN: 978-1-63731-637-5

Printed and bound in the USA.
NinjaLifeHacks.tv

Ninja Life Hacks®
by Mary Nhin

NINJAS
Go to Work
A Rhyming Children's Book for Career Day

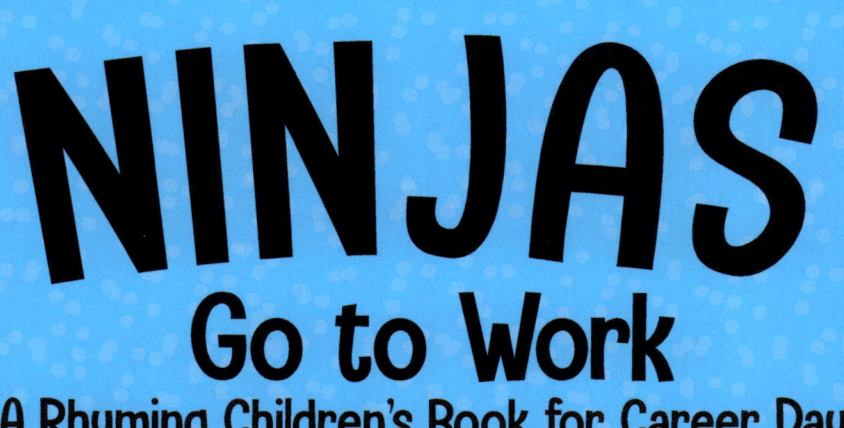

Ninja Life Hacks
by Mary Nhin

My friends and I were dreaming
Of what we could be.
Will we be actors? Bus drivers? Artists?
Or perhaps we'll work under the sea?

'Astronaut!' one yells. 'Up in space!
Floating around the stars.
And perhaps I'll catch some aliens
In alien-catching jars!'

There was so much to do at the fire station.
The firefighters were busy.
And after sliding down the firepole,
I felt real dizzy!

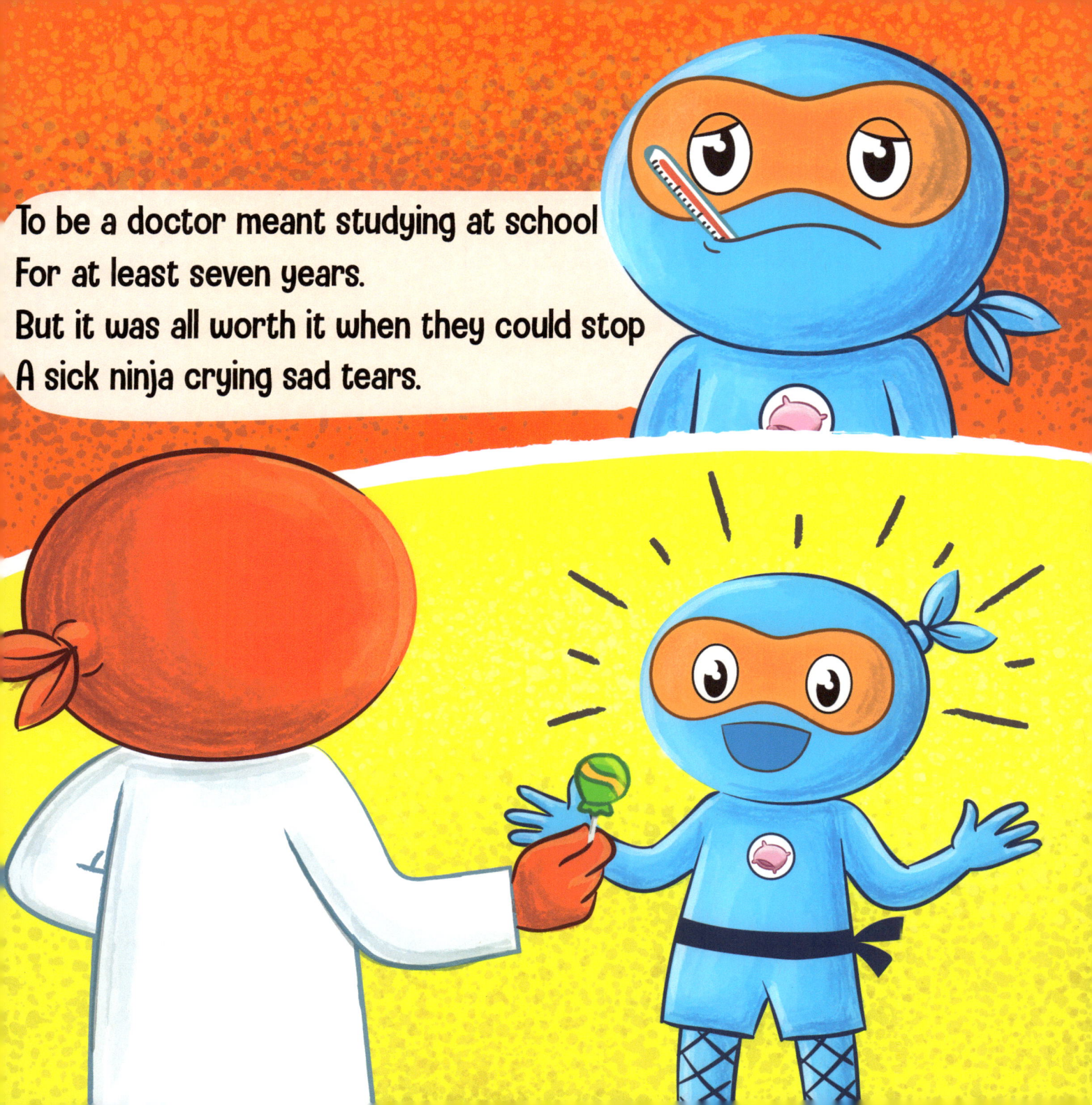

Scientist ninjas did experiments
Wanting to make the world better.
While postal workers travel around the world
Delivering every letter.

Then all of my friends gave me a hug,
And said, "There's no need to fuss.
Do you know why we all love working hard?
Because **you** set the example for us!"

Continue the learning with our lesson plans at ninjalifehacks.tv

 @marynhin @officialninjalifehacks
#NinjaLifeHacks

 Ninja Life Hacks

 Mary Nhin   Ninja Life Hacks

 @officialninjalifehacks

www.ingramcontent.com/pod-product-compliance
Lightning Source LLC
Chambersburg PA
CBHW041106070526
44583CB00002B/78